The Standard

By Shareta Cunningham

AITactiX Publishing Group

Published by AITactiX Publishing Group
First edition: 2026

To God —
who planted the vision before I even had the words,
who kept the fire burning when I was ready to walk away,
and who reminded me, over and over again,
that everything I was already designed on purpose.
To my family & friends-
always supporting whatever I do.
Much Love!

Contents

CHAPTER 1

You Were Never the Problem

Stop trying to fit into a mold that wasn't built for your soul. You weren't born broken; you were born into a world that couldn't handle your volume.

You Were Never the Problem

The most dangerous woman in the room is the one who finally knows her worth. You feel me? So, how are you feeling?

If you're anything like the women I talk to every day, you're feeling a little tired. You're tired of the performance. You're tired of checking the boxes and still feeling like the math of your life doesn't add up to fulfillment. You trying to be the best version of what everyone else needed you to be—the perfect mother, the reliable employee, the supportive partner, the woman who makes everyone else feel comfortable while she slowly suffocates in the background.

You've been told that if you just adjusted your volume, softened your edges, or dimmed your light a little bit, you'd finally find that peace you're looking for. But here is the contrarian truth that no one wanted to tell you: You were never the problem. You weren't too loud, too stubborn, or too difficult. You were simply too much for people who were committed to playing small. We are going to dismantle every lie you've been sold about your value, starting right now. This isn't a makeover. It's a reclaiming.

Wanted vs. Desirable Truth: Desirability has nothing to do with being wanted.

We have to clear the air about this word "desirable." In our culture, especially for women over forty, we've been conditioned to believe that being desirable is a passive state. We think it means being chosen, being sought after, or being "wanted" by a man, a company, or a social circle. We've been sold the idea that our desirability is a grade given to us by an outside audience.

Let me tell you something: that's a lie designed to keep you performing.

Being "wanted" is about their appetite. Being "desirable" is about your essence. Real desirability has nothing to do with who is looking at you and everything to do with how you look at yourself. It's about how much you want your own life, your own presence, your own energy, and your own future. When I say I am a desired woman, I'm not talking about a line of suitors at the door—though they may come. I'm talking about the fact that I actually want to be in my own skin. I am desired by *me.*

Most women spend their entire lives trying to be "wanted." They curate their bodies, their personalities, and their schedules to fit someone else's preference. But when you live your life to be wanted, you are always at the mercy of the person doing the wanting. If they change their mind, your value drops. If they leave, your worth goes out the door with them.

I had to learn this the hard way. I spent years in rooms where I felt I had to humble myself, where I had to be quiet just to keep the peace. I thought that by making myself useful and wanted, I was building worth. I wasn't. I was building a cage. Real desirability is silent. It doesn't post for validation. It doesn't ask, "Do you like me?" It simply states, "I am here, and I am enough." When your peace stops depending on who shows up for you, you become harder to shake and easier to read. You stop being a reaction to other people, and start being a decision you made about yourself.

The Assigned Version of You: Who told you what you were worth — and why you benefited from the lie

I want you to think back to the very first time you felt like you weren't enough. Maybe it was a comment from a parent, a look from a teacher, or the way a partner handled your heart. Somewhere along the line, someone handed you a script. They assigned you a version of yourself that was manageable, convenient, and safe. And because you were a good student of life, you believed them.

We accept these assigned identities because they offer us a false sense of security. If we play the role, we think we'll be loved. If we follow the rules, we think we'll be protected. But you've reached an age now where you can see that the protection was an illusion. You followed the rules, and you still got hurt. You played the role, and you still ended up feeling empty.

Who told you that having high standards was a trauma response? Who told you that being selective about who gets your time was "acting brand new"? Therapy culture likes to tell us that our boundaries are just walls built by our wounds. I disagree. Being selective is not trauma; it's taste. Knowing exactly what you will and will not accept is not a defense mechanism; it's discernment.

You have to ask yourself: Who benefits from you staying in the version of yourself that doesn't believe in her own power? Usually, it's the people who are using your light to brighten their own dark corners. They need you to stay "humble" so they don't have to face their own insecurities.

I learned that I don't need validation from anyone. I just need to be my authentic self and love me for who I am and who I am about to become. You have been carrying around a version of yourself that was never yours to begin with. It's time to put it down. It's heavy, it's outdated, and it's dragging you away from your destiny.

Too Much Was Always Enough: Being "a lot" was never the problem

How many times have you been told you're "a lot"? Or that you're "too much"? Too ambitious, too sensitive, too opinionated, too much of a handful?

Let's set the record straight: "Too much" is just a label

used by people who don't have enough capacity to hold you. If you go to a small glass with a gallon of water, the glass is going to overflow. That's not the water's fault. That's the glass's limitation. You've been trying to pour your gallon-sized soul into shot-glass-sized relationships and wondering why everyone is getting wet and angry.

Being "a lot" was never the problem. The problem was the container.

For a long time, I thought I had to mute myself so others could be heard. I thought that to be a "good" person, I had to keep meeting people where they were—even if that meant swallowing my own voice to make room for theirs. But the right people, the right opportunities, and the right rooms will never need you to whisper. The right people will hand you the microphone and ask you to turn it up.

You have to stop apologizing for your volume. Your passion is not a defect. Your standards are not an insult to others. Your presence is a gift that requires a certain level of maturity to appreciate. When I realized that I didn't mind being someone's shoulder to lean on, but I refused to be their doormat, everything changed. I realized there are women just like you who are looking up, waiting for someone to give them permission to be their full selves.

You are the standard. You aren't reaching for it; you are it. And if people can't meet that standard, they aren't your people. It's that simple. It's not cold; it's clear. When you finally accept that you were never the problem, you stop looking for solutions in other people and start looking for them in the mirror.

Takeaway

Your worth is not a performance, and it's certainly not a negotiation. You have been fighting a battle that was never yours to win because the game was rigged from the start. You were trying to find value in a system that only values your compliance.

Now that you know the truth—that you were never the problem—we can finally stop the demolition and start the construction. But before we build the new, we have to see the old for what it really is. In the next chapter, we're going to look at what real self-worth looks like when the cameras are off and the doors are closed. We're going to talk about the work nobody talks about.

You feel me? Let's get to work.

CHAPTER 2

The Work Nobody Talks About

Real self-worth doesn't post for validation or wait for permission; it's the quiet, steady decision to value yourself before you have a single reason to prove it.

The Work Nobody Talks About

If you have to post it to prove it, you don't own it yet. I know that's not what the influencers told you, but we're here for the truth, not the trend. We live in a world that thrives on the noise of self-promotion. We've been conditioned to believe that if we aren't shouting our worth from the digital rooftops or wearing our confidence like a neon sign, then we must not have any. But let me tell you something: the loudest person in the room is rarely the most secure. Real self-worth? It doesn't perform. It doesn't flinch. It doesn't need a crowd to confirm it's beautiful, and it doesn't need a title to confirm its powerful.

I've been the woman who sought validation in the eyes of others. I've been the one who thought if I could just perform well enough, serve enough, and stay quiet enough, I would finally earn the right to be respected. I learned the hard way that when you build your value on the opinions of people, you give them the power to devalue you at a discount. You feel me? The work nobody talks about isn't about a bubble bath or a shopping spree. It's about the brutal, beautiful process of stripping away everything you were told you needed to be, so you can finally see who you actually are. It's not a makeover. It's a dismantling.

Affirmations Aren't Enough Truth

You've heard it a thousand times: "Stand in the mirror and tell yourself you're a queen." Look, I'm all for speaking life into yourself, but affirmations without alignment are just lies you tell your reflection. If you're standing there saying "I am rich" while you're operating from a poverty mindset, your spirit knows you're fronting. If you're saying "I am loved" but you're still entertaining people who treat you like an option, those words are just noise.

Self-worth that needs proof isn't self-worth—it's a performance. When we spend our energy trying to convince others (and ourselves) that we have value, we are actually operating from a place of deficit. We are performing for an audience that we shouldn't even have invited to the show. The truth is, if you have to prove it, you're still trying to earn it. And you cannot earn something that was yours by birthright.

You have to stop looking for the "proof" of your value in your bank account, your relationship status, or your dress size. Those are just accessories. They are not the essence. I had to learn to humble myself, be quiet, and realize that I didn't need an amen from the crowd to know the sermon was good. You have to get to a point where your worth is so non-negotiable that it doesn't even occur to you to ask for a second opinion. When you stop performing, you start living. And let me tell you, the freedom on the other side of that performance is the most expensive thing you'll ever own.

Doing the Thing Before You Feel Ready

Waiting for confidence is the greatest trap ever set for a woman. We've been sold this idea that one day we'll wake up feeling 100% prepared, fearless, and "ready" to take our seat at the table. That day is a myth. Confidence is not a feeling that drops out of the sky; it's a decision you make in the middle of the mess.

You don't build confidence by thinking; you build it by doing. You take the step while your knees are shaking. You launch the business while you're still learning the industry. You set the boundary while your heart is pounding. For a long time, I thought I had to have all the answers before I could speak my truth. I thought I had to be "perfected" before I could be THE STANDARD. But I realized that the version of me that was struggling, the version that was misunderstood, she was the one who had the most to offer.

Stop waiting for the permission slip. Stop waiting for the fear to vanish. Fear doesn't go away; it just gets used to the backseat while you drive the car. When you do the thing before you're ready, you're telling your subconscious that your purpose is more important than your comfort. That is how you build a spine of steel. You don't need to feel ready to be worthy. You just need to show up.

The Real Work

The real work doesn't happen on stage. It doesn't happen under the lights or in the middle of the celebration. The real work happens in the room where nobody is watching. It's in the quiet moments at 3:00 AM when you have to choose to forgive yourself for what you didn't know then. It's in the grocery store when you see someone who hurt you and you choose to keep your peace instead of losing your cool. It's in the daily, boring, repetitive choices to honor your own word to yourself.

Most people want the crown, but they don't want the crushing that makes the oil. They want the title, but they don't want the transformation that happens in the silence. I've had to learn that being my authentic self-meant I would be misunderstood by some—and I had to be okay with that. I had to realize that if I'm "too much" for some people, they aren't my people. That's not a loss; that's a narrowing.

The real work is about becoming a woman who is so deeply rooted in her own energy that she doesn't need to suck the oxygen out of the room to feel seen. It's about being a shoulder for others because you know what it's like to have none but also knowing when to step back and protect your own peace. This is the work of an "upgrade," not a "comeback." You aren't trying to get back to who you were before the world broke your heart. You are arriving as the woman who was forged in that fire. She is sharper. She is more edited. She is intentional. She is you.

Takeaway

Real worth is a private victory before it is ever a public reality. Stop performing for the people who aren't even in your league and start honoring the woman in the mirror. You don't need a witness to be valid. You feel me? So, how are you feeling? Now that you know the work is internal, it's time to talk about how we filter who gets access to this new version of you. Next, we're going to get into why your "high standards" aren't a problem—they're your protection.

CHAPTER 3

Discernment Is Not Damage

Stop apologizing for the velvet ropes around your energy; having a high standard isn't a symptom of your past—it is the proof of your presence.

Discernment Is Not Damage

The world will try to convince you that your boundaries are actually scars. They want to look at your high standards, your refusal to settle, and your quiet 'no' and label it as 'unresolved trauma.' They'll say you're being guarded because you've been hurt, or that you're being difficult because you're defensive. But let me tell you something: knowing exactly what you will and will not accept is not a defense mechanism. It's discernment. It is the most powerful tool a woman over forty has in her arsenal. You've lived enough, seen enough, and survived enough to know the difference between a golden opportunity and a gilded cage. You aren't 'damaged' because you don't let just anyone into your space anymore; you are simply finally paying attention to the cost of admission. You feel me?

High Standards Are Not Trauma: Being Selective Is Taste

Modern therapy culture has a way of pathologizing a woman's power. If you decide you don't want to date a man who doesn't have his life in order, they call it 'avoidant attachment.' If you decide to cut off a friend who constantly drains your energy, they call it 'hyper-independence.' They want to find a wound for every boundary you set. But what if it's not a wound? What if it's just taste?

Think about it like this: When you go to a fine-dining

restaurant, you expect the silver to be polished, the wine to be the right temperature, and the service to be impeccable. You aren't being 'difficult' when you send back a cold steak; you are simply maintaining the standard of the establishment you're paying for. Your life is the most exclusive establishment on the planet. Why would you lower the menu just because someone can't afford the bill?

I've spent years learning that being selective is not a trauma response—it's a vibration. When I was younger, I thought I had to be accessible to everyone to prove I was 'good' or 'humane.' I thought my worth was tied to how much I could endure. But the woman I am today—the one who has arrived on the other side of the fire—knows that my selectivity is actually my sanity. It's about how much I want my own life. It's about loving my own energy enough to protect it from those who only know how to consume.

You have to stop explaining your 'why' to people who don't even have the capacity to understand your 'what.' If someone calls you 'picky' or 'high maintenance,' let them. Maintenance is required for things of high value. You don't see a Ferrari owner apologizing for the cost of the premium fuel, do you? Your standards are not a reflection of what you've been through; they are a reflection of where you are going. You aren't building walls; you're building a sanctuary. And in a sanctuary, not everything is allowed inside.

The Front Row Seat: Not Everyone Deserves Access

We have to talk about the 'front row.' In the theater of your life, the front row is that intimate space where people see your tears, hear your rawest dreams, and feel your most vulnerable energy. For too long, you've been letting people sit in the front row who only bought a ticket for the back balcony. You've been giving premium access to people with general admission mindsets.

Real self-worth doesn't announce itself. It doesn't post for validation, and it definitely doesn't audition for love. I had to lose myself a few times to learn that. I had to realize I don't need anyone's permission to be myself—I just need to show up as who I am and love the woman I'm becoming. That shift changed how I handed out 'front row' seats. I started realizing that some people were only there to watch the show, not to support the star.

Discernment is the gatekeeper that asks: *Does this person bring peace or do they bring problems? Does this opportunity expand me, or does it extract from me?* If the answer isn't clear, the door stays shut. This isn't about being mean or acting 'better than.' It's about stewardship. You are the steward of your soul. If you let people into your inner circle who haven't earned the right to be there, you aren't being 'kind'—you're being irresponsible with your own spirit.

You don't owe anyone a seat at your table just because

you've known them for ten years. You don't owe anyone your time just because they're family. Access is earned through consistency, respect, and a shared frequency. If they can't meet the standard, they can watch from the street. You have to be okay with the silence that comes when you stop inviting the wrong people in. Most women are terrified of that silence, so they fill it with noise just to feel 'wanted.' But remember being desired isn't about being wanted by them. It's about how much you want your own presence. When you start wanting yourself, the guest list for your life gets a lot shorter, and that's a beautiful thing.

The Right Ones Won't Ask You to Shrink

There is a specific kind of pressure we face as women to bend ourselves into whatever shape makes other people comfortable. It sounds noble, doesn't it? It sounds like empathy. But in reality, it's often a trap designed to make us soften, adjust, and apologize for our own growth so that others don't have to confront their own stillness. We are told to dim our light, so we don't hurt their eyes.

I'm here to tell you: stop shrinking. If they can't see you, let them get some glasses.

The right people, the right opportunities, and the right rooms will never require you to be less than what you are. They will never ask you to quiet your voice or humble your ambition to make them feel more secure. When I finally stepped into my role as THE STANDARD, I realized that the people who truly belonged in my life were the ones who were inspired by my volume, not intimidated by it. They didn't need me to be small so they could feel big.

Discernment allows you to spot the 'shrinkers' from a mile away. You know the ones—they give backhanded compliments, they get quiet when you have a win, or they always remind you of 'the old you' whenever you start acting like the 'new you.' Those people are not your tribe. They are your anchors. And you were born to sail.

When you stop dimming yourself down, something miraculous happens you become a magnet for the people who are actually on your level. You stop attracting projects that drain you and start attracting partnerships that pour into you. You realize that you don't have to 'search' for your place—you carry your place with you. You are the room. You are the standard. And anyone who asks you to compromise that is simply telling you that they don't belong in your space. Don't be mad at them for not being able to handle you; just be grateful your discernment caught it before you wasted another year trying to fit into their tiny box.

Takeaway

Your standards are your crown, not your cage. Stop apologizing for the 'no' that protects your 'yes.' Discernment isn't a sign that you're broken; it's the proof that you've finally decided to value the woman you've become over the woman you used to be. You didn't just survive the past; you learned from it, and now you're applying the lessons. Keep your circle tight and your standards high.

Now that we've cleared the room of the wrong energy, it's time to talk about what happens when the floor falls out from under you. Because holding the standard is easy when things are good—but what happens when everything falls apart? In the next chapter, we're going to talk about why the most dangerous woman in the room is the one who refuses to drop her crown, even in the middle of a storm.

CHAPTER 4

Still She Stands

Rock bottom isn't a graveyard; it's the foundation for a structure that can actually withstand your weight. Holding the standard when your world collapses is the ultimate proof that your worth was never tied to your circumstances.

Still, She Stands

Rock bottom is the only place where the view is completely honest. You've been there, haven't you? That moment when the floor you spent years building suddenly gives way, and you're falling through the air, wondering which of your beautiful things is going to break first. Maybe it was the marriage you thought would last forever. Maybe it was the career that defined you, or the friend you trusted with the secrets you didn't even tell yourself. When those things crumble, the world expects you to crumble with them. The world expects you to look for a shovel and start digging your way back to where you used to be.

But I need you to hear me clearly: the most dangerous woman in the room is the one who has seen it all fall apart and didn't lose her mind because she finally found herself. You feel me? So, how are you feeling? If you're standing in the middle of a mess right now, I want you to stop trying to clean it up for five minutes. I want you to look at the rubble and realize that if it could be shaken, it wasn't meant to stay. Still, she stands. Not because she's bulletproofed, and not because she didn't cry, but because she decided that her standard was not negotiable, even when her life was unrecognizable.

When She Came Undone

There is a specific kind of silence that follows a collapse. It's the silence of the phone not ringing, the silence of an empty house, or the silence of your own voice when you realize you've been lying to yourself for years. This is the chapter nobody wants to write, but it's the one everyone needs to read because we've been conditioned to believe that 'undone' is a bad thing. We've been told that a woman who loses her cool, her relationship, or her status is a woman who has failed.

I've lived that life. I've been in those rooms where people misunderstood my truth and I had to learn the hard way that sometimes; you just have to humble yourself and be quiet. Not because you're defeated, but because the truth doesn't need to shout to be true. When I came undone, I realized I had been carrying a version of myself that was designed to make everyone else comfortable. I was the 'reliable' one, the 'strong' one, the one who always had the answer. When I finally hit the ground, I realized that the version of me I was trying so hard to save was actually the one holding me back.

Coming undone is a gift. It's the stripping away of the performance. We spend so much energy trying to prove our worth through our roles—as wives, mothers, bosses, or daughters—that we forget that worth is inherent. If you need a title to feel significant, you aren't significant yet. When everything is stripped away and you are standing there with nothing but your breath and your heartbeat, that is when you find out if you actually like the woman you are. If you don't, that's where the work begins. But if you can stand in the wreckage and still tell yourself, "I made it, and I am still whole," then you've found a kind of power nothing can touch. You stop needing the crowd to clap when your own spirit already stands and applauds.

She Let Him Go

We stay too long because we're afraid of the void. We stay in dead-end relationships, toxic partnerships, and draining friendships because we think the 'emptiness' that follows will swallow us whole. We've been sold this lie that being desired means being wanted by someone else. But I told you before: desirability is about how much you want your own life. When she finally let him go—whether that 'him' was a man, a job, or an old version of herself—the world didn't end. It began.

I learned that being selective is not trauma; it's taste. There were times I had to realize that I didn't need a seat at every table, especially the ones where I had to shrink myself just to fit in the chair. You know the feeling. You're at dinner, or in a meeting, and you feel that little tug in your spirit telling you to dim your light so you don't blind the person across from you. You soften your voice. You adjust your standards. You accept the 'good enough' because you're terrified of the 'nothing.'

Let me tell you something: the 'nothing' is where the magic happens. When you let go of what is no longer serving your highest self, you aren't creating a hole; you're creating a space. And God, or the Universe, or whatever you call that higher power, cannot fill a space that is already cluttered with trash. Letting go is an act of supreme discernment. It's saying, 'I recognize that this relationship has reached its expiration date, and I am not a dumpster for old energy.' The moment you stop holding onto the wrong things is the moment your hands become free to catch the right ones. And the right people? They won't need you to dim down. They'll bring their own sunglasses.

The Upgrade

Culture loves a comeback story. They love to see the woman who was cheated on, walked out on, or fired, return to her former glory. But I don't believe in comebacks. A comeback implies you're returning to the person you were before the fire. Why would you want to do that? That woman was the one who got burned.

Rebuilding after loss is not a comeback; it's an upgrade. The woman on the other side of betrayal or rock bottom is not the same woman who went in. She is sharper. She is more edited. She is intentional. She didn't come back—she arrived. When you go through the fire, you lose the extra weight. You lose the people-pleasing, you lose the need for outside applause, and you lose the delusion that you are responsible for everyone else's happiness.

This is what it means to be THE STANDARD. You don't just survive the storm; you use the wind to clear the path. You realize that your self-worth doesn't need to be proved—it just needs to be lived. People will see you standing after the collapse and they'll ask, 'How did she do it?' They'll expect you to be bitter, or broken, or loud about your pain. But your silence will be your greatest testimony. When you know who you are, you don't have to explain the upgrade. You just live in it. You move into the new house of your life, you decorate it with high standards and velvet-rope boundaries, and you never look back at the rubble with anything but gratitude. Because the rubble taught you that you were the building, not the bricks.

Takeaway

Your value is not a variable; it is a constant. When your world falls apart, it's not a sign that you failed—it's a sign that you've outgrown your current containers. Don't look for a comeback; look for the upgrade. Still, she stands, not because the world was kind, but because she became her own foundation. Now that the ground is clear, it's time to show them what a woman who finally knows her worth can actually build. You feel me?

CHAPTER 5

She Is the Standard

Stop waiting for a seat at the table when you are the entire banquet; the moment you decide your worth is non-negotiable, the world has no choice but to adjust to your frequency.

She Is the Standard

There is a specific kind of silence that happens when a woman who knows exactly who she is walks into a room. It isn't the silence of intimidation; it's the silence of recognition. The air shifts. The frequency changes. People stop looking at their phones and start looking at the way you carry your own atmosphere. You aren't auditioning for a role, and you aren't hunting for a compliment. You are simply existing in the fullness of your choice. Most women spend their lives walking into rooms wondering if the room likes them. The Standard walks into a room and decides whether she likes the room. You feel me?

Living as The Standard isn't a mask you put on for the public or a performance you give when the cameras are on. It is the steady, quiet, unbothered rhythm of your daily life. It's what you do when no one is watching, when the only person you have to answer to is the woman looking back at you in the mirror. You've spent forty-plus years being what the world needed you to be—the daughter, the mother, the employee, the peacekeeper. Now, it's time to be the woman you decided to be. It's time to stop auditing your existence and start owning your throne.

The Room Changes When You Enter

Your standard is contagious. I need you to understand that

when you elevate your energy, you aren't just helping yourself—you are giving every other woman in that room a silent permission slip to do the same. We have been lied to, told that our strength is a threat and our confidence is "too much." But let me tell you something: you can never be "too much" for someone who has the capacity to handle greatness. If they are intimidated, that is their inner work to do, not yours to fix.

When I talk about the room changing, I'm talking about the power of presence. Presence is what happens when your internal value matches your external expression. You don't have to raise your voice to make a point. You don't have to explain your boundaries twice. When you are the standard, your "NO" is a complete sentence and your "YES" is a premium offering. People start to treat you differently not because you've asked them to, but because they can feel that you won't accept anything less. You are setting the thermostat for every interaction you have.

Think about the doors you used to stand outside of, hoping someone would let you in. Now I want you to realize you're not looking for an entry point anymore—you're the one who decides what gets built. If a room can't hold the size of your growth, you don't rearrange yourself to fit its dimensions; you walk out and find a space with higher ceilings. This isn't arrogance—it's accuracy. It's recognizing that your time, your energy, and your peace are high-value assets. If the room doesn't respect the asset, the asset leaves the room. That's how you change the game.

Building the Brand of You

Your life is your greatest creative project. I often talk about being a brand architect, but I'm not talking about logos, website colors, or social media aesthetics. I'm talking about the Brand of You. What is the promise you make to yourself every morning? What is the energy people feel when they think of your name? When you decide that you are the standard, every choice you make—from the way you drink your water to the way you curate your inner circle—becomes an act of branding.

We are taught to build brands for businesses, but we neglect the brand of our soul. The Brand of You means you are intentional about what you allow into your space. You wouldn't put cheap, toxic materials into a luxury build, would you? So why are you putting cheap thoughts and toxic people into a luxury life? You are a masterpiece in progress, a purple-and-gold crown in a world of cardboard cutouts. To build this brand, you have to be willing to be your own most ruthless editor. You have to cut out the scenes that don't serve the storyline of the woman you are becoming.

This is where it gets real. Building the Brand of You means you stop being a generalist and you become a specialist in your own joy. You stop trying to please everybody because a brand that appeals to everyone is a brand that stands for nothing. Be distinct. Be specific. Be unapologetic about your tastes and your requirements. If you prefer the finer things—the finer conversations, the finer friendships, the finer peace—then demand them. Not out of vanity, but out of a deep-seated knowledge that you are worth the investment. Your life is a curated experience. Make sure you're the one holding the gallery keys.

The Decision

This is the final chapter of your old life and the first day of your new reality. The shift doesn't happen when you get the promotion, find the partner, or lose the weight. The shift happens the moment you make The Decision. What is The Decision? It is the internal vow that you will never again negotiate with your own worth. It is the moment you stop asking, "Am I desired?" and start asking, "Do I desire this life?"

I've been there. I've been in the place where I felt misunderstood, where I felt like I had to dim my light so others wouldn't have to squint. But then I realized that my light wasn't the problem—their eyes were. I had to humble myself not by making myself small, but by recognizing that my validation didn't come from their applause. It came from God, and it came from the truth of who I was born to be. Once you make that decision, the weight of everyone else's opinion just falls off. It's like taking off an old, heavy coat that never fit you anyway.

You are not a comeback story. A comeback implies you're trying to return to a version of yourself that didn't work. No, baby, you are an upgrade. You are the version 2.0, 3.0, 5.0. The woman who survived the heartbreak, the betrayal, and the loss is not the woman who is standing here today. She is sharper. She is more edited. She is more intentional. She didn't just come back; she arrived. And now that you've arrived, what are you going to do with all that power?

Takeaway

Living as The Standard means you stop auditioning for your own life and start directing it. It's the realization that you are the reward, not the one seeking it. Your worth is a settled matter, an absolute truth that doesn't require a single person's agreement. Now that you've claimed your crown, it's time to learn how to walk in the silence that speaks louder than words.

CHAPTER 6

The Silence That Speaks

When you stop explaining your value to people who aren't even qualified to assess it, you don't just find peace—you find power. Your silence isn't a lack of words; it's a high-grade filter for your future.

The Silence That Speaks

The most dangerous woman in the room isn't the one talking the loudest; she's the one who doesn't feel the need to talk at all. You feel me? We have been conditioned to believe that if we aren't defending our choices, if we aren't justifying our boundaries, or if we aren't constantly over-communicating our worth, then we are being misunderstood. But let me tell you something: being misunderstood by the wrong people is actually a spiritual promotion.

I used to think I had to win every argument and make sure everyone saw my heart. I'd spend hours—precious hours I'll never get back—trying to get people to understand why I did what I did or why I said what I said. I was exhausted. I was leaking energy like a faucet that nobody bothered to turn off. Then I realized the truth: a woman who knows her worth doesn't have a lot to say to people who aren't committed to hearing her. Real self-worth keeps its own counsel. It doesn't beg for likes, and it doesn't chase applause from people who were never paying attention in the first place. When you finally step into your authority, you realize that your silence is often the loudest thing about you. It's the sound of a woman who has nothing left to prove. This is where the real shift happens. It's not about what you start doing to build your life; it's about what you have the courage to stop doing.

She Stopped Explaining Herself

There is a specific kind of freedom that comes when you stop giving out a syllabus for your life. Most of us have been taught that if we set a boundary, we owe someone a thirty-minute presentation on why that boundary exists. If we don't want to go to the party, we make up a lie or a long-winded excuse because we think "No" is a dirty word. Honey, "No" is a complete sentence. I used to over-explain myself into exhaustion, thinking if I justified my truth enough, people would finally understand it. But discernment taught me better—I don't owe anyone a paragraph for a decision that's already final. Knowing exactly what you will and will not accept is not a defense mechanism—it's taste. When you stop explaining yourself, you are essentially saying, "I don't need you to agree with my reality for it to be real."

Think about the energy you waste trying to convince a $2 person that you are $100. They don't have the currency to handle you, so why are you still at the register? When you stop explaining, you reclaim your time. You stop letting people into the inner court of your mind. You begin to realize that your reasons are private property. If you choose to move, move. If you choose to change your mind, change it. If you choose to walk away from a relationship that was draining your soul, you don't owe the person who drained you a roadmap of your exit. The standard is this: those who belong in your life will understand your heart without a manual, and those who don't won't understand it even if you write it in the sky. Stop talking and start being. Let your results be your noise.

She Stopped Shrinking at the Table

How many times have you walked into a room and immediately felt the urge to pull your shoulders in? We've been told to encounter people "where they are," but we've misinterpreted that to mean we have to lower our frequency to make them feel comfortable. We dim the lights so their eyes don't hurt. We soften our tone, so we don't sound "too aggressive." We shrink our dreams, so they don't look too big for the small-minded people we're sitting next to.

Let me be direct: the right people will never require you to be less. If the room feels tight, it's not because you're too big; it's because the room is too small for the woman you are becoming. I've been in those spaces where people misunderstood my confidence for arrogance. I used to think I needed to stay quiet to keep the peace. But I realized that I was keeping the peace for everyone else while starting a war inside my own spirit.

When you stop apologizing for your own growth, you give others permission to rise with you—or the opportunity to fall away. Either way, you win. You are the entire banquet, so stop acting like you're just grateful for a seat. If someone is intimidated by your light, that's their shadow work to do, not yours. You are not responsible for the insecurities of others. Your only responsibility is to show up as your most unapologetic, authentic self. This is what it means to be THE STANDARD. You set the tone. You define the energy. If they can't meet you at your level, it isn't your job to go down to the basement to get them. Love them from the balcony and keep it moving.

She Stopped Waiting to Be Chosen

This is the big one. Remember this lie that desirability means being wanted by someone else—a partner, an employer, a social circle. We measure our worth by how many people raise their hand for us, instead of how fully we show up for ourselves. We spend our lives waiting for someone to pick us, to choose us, to validate that we are "Enough."

Desirability was never about someone else's want? It's about how much you crave your own life. It's about how much you're drawn to your own energy. When you stop waiting on an invitation, you realize you were never on the guest list to begin with—you were the host all along.

In my own journey, I had to realize validation was never the prize. The real win was building a life I actually wanted to live in, regardless of who noticed. That shift changes everything. You no longer walk into a room wondering if they like you; you walk into a room wondering if they're worth your time. You stop waiting for a role and start writing the script.

When you choose yourself, the world has no choice but to follow suit. This isn't about being cold; it's about being intentional. It's about looking at your reflection and saying, "I'm the one I've been waiting for." You stop chasing opportunities and start attracting them because your frequency is tuned to "Chosen." You are no longer an option. You are the priority. And when you live like that, the silence stops being a lack of sound and starts being a symphony of self-assurance.

Takeaway

Your power isn't in your ability to convince the world of your value; it's in your refusal to bargain for it. When you stop explaining, stop shrinking, and stop waiting for a green light from others, you finally start living. Silence isn't empty; it's full of the answers you've been looking for. Now that you've cleared the noise, it's time to listen to the one voice that actually knows the way. So, how are you feeling? Are you ready to trust the wisdom that's been living in your bones since the beginning?

CHAPTER 7

Her Body Knew First

Your body has its own frequency, its own logic, and its own survival kit—learn to stop negotiating with the gut feelings that were designed to save you. You don't need a second opinion when your spirit already said 'no.'

Her Body Knew First

How many times have you stood in a room with someone who looked perfect on paper, while your stomach twisted like old wire? You had every reason to say yes—the resume checked out, the logic added up, the room itself was pressuring you to comply. But that tightness in your chest, that breath you couldn't quite catch—that was your body choosing you before your mind got the chance to talk you out of it. We've been trained to trust a spreadsheet over a shiver, to rank logic above the language we were born speaking. But the Standard isn't built on what you can justify. It's built on what your body already confirmed. Your body is the most loyal advisor you'll ever have, and it has never once lied to you.

The Intuition She Ignored

Stop calling it a "hunch." Stop calling it a "vibe." Call it what it is: information your body collected before your mind caught up. Every season of my life where I felt lost or drained, the issue was never that I lacked information. I had it. I just refused to act on it, because acting on it meant choosing myself over the comfort of staying in something familiar. I wanted the relationship to work, so I overrode the ache in my chest. I wanted the deal to be real, so I explained away the headache. I silenced my own alarm system so I could keep chasing something that was already gone.

We've all done it. We pay people to hand back the answers we've been sitting on the entire time. If you need three friends to weigh in on whether a man is right for you, you already know he isn't—you're just looking for someone to give you permission to leave. If you have to talk yourself into excitement about a project, you've already moved on; you're just stalling the goodbye.

The Standard means you stop outsourcing what's already yours. You were born with a compass older than your trauma and sharper than your intellect. Ignoring it isn't rational—its self-abandonment dressed up as patience. I had to learn that every time I overrode my own gut, I was choosing someone else's comfort over my own clarity. Not anymore. From here forward: if it's not an immediate yes in my spirit, it's a no in my life. No further conversation needed.

Rest Is Not Laziness — It Is Strategy

A lie told: that the Standard means proving how much you can carry. We wear exhaustion like a medal, convinced that if we're not running on empty, we're not doing enough. Here's the truth: a depleted woman is an easy woman to move. When you're running on fumes, you don't have the energy left to hold your own line. You start letting things slide that you'd never tolerate at full strength.

Rest isn't a reward you earn—it's the foundation your

authority stands on. I used to think being endlessly available made me strong. It didn't. Carrying everyone else while my own back was breaking wasn't leadership; it was self-neglect with a good outfit on. I choose myself now, which means I choose rest before depletion forces my hand.

Productivity isn't proving your stamina. Productivity is closing the laptop when you're done. It's saying, "I don't have the bandwidth for this conversation today," and meaning it. When you're actually rested, you walk into rooms with a stillness that commands attention without a single word. You're not chasing outcomes—you're already complete. You are the banquet. And the banquet has never once rushed itself to satisfy a guest who showed up uninvited.

Her Nervous System Is Part of the Standard Too

You've heard "it's just business" or "don't take it personally." That's language designed to talk you out of your own instincts. Everything is personal when it's happening to your one life. Your nervous system isn't an inconvenience to manage—it's the gatekeeper deciding what gets access to you. If a room makes you feel like you have to soften your edges to be tolerated, that room isn't safe for your biology, no matter how good it looks from the outside.

I've trained myself to listen to how my body responds before I listen to anyone's explanation. Sometimes you don't need to confront the room—you just need to leave it.

Silence is a filter, not a weakness. If your pulse spikes when a name lights up your phone, that's not anticipation. That's a warning. The Standard doesn't negotiate with warnings. It exits.

Rebuilding after loss or betrayal was never about recovering the woman you used to be. She's gone, and she's not coming back—good. The woman arriving now is one who treats her own peace as non-negotiable. You don't have to work at being authentic. You simply stop making room for anything that asks you to perform. When your nervous system is regulated, you stop reacting to the world and start setting the terms for it. You are the frequency the room adjusts to, not the other way around.

Takeaway

Your body is the only home you'll ever fully own—stop treating its signals like suggestions and start treating them like law. The Standard isn't a mindset exercise. It's a daily decision to choose yourself before anyone else gets a vote. You didn't just survive what tried to silence you. You listened, you chose yourself, and you arrived.

CHAPTER 8

The Woman She Was Becoming

Stop looking for your lost self in the rearview mirror; the woman you are becoming wasn't lost, she was waiting for you to stop settling for the version everyone else was comfortable with. Identity is not found—it is built.

The Woman She Was Becoming

Stop looking for the woman you used to be. Seriously. Stop digging through the archives of your life trying to find that girl who was "easier" to deal with, more "compliant," or more "relatable." She's gone, and frankly, she didn't have the tools to survive where you're headed. You've been told that finding yourself is a scavenger hunt, like you're searching for some buried treasure under the layers of life's debris. But here is the truth that will change your entire frequency: Identity is not found—it is built.

You don't find yourself; you decide yourself. You don't discover your worth; you establish it. Most women spend forty years trying to get back to a version of themselves that was never actually whole to begin with. They want the girl before the heartbreak, the girl before the disappointment, the girl before the world told her she was too much. But that girl was fragile. The woman you are becoming now? She's something else entirely. She is sharper, more edited, more intentional, and she doesn't arrive by accident. She is the result of every 'no' you finally had the courage to say. She is the architecture you built on top of the rock bottom you survived. When you finally realize that the blueprint is in your hands, you stop asking for permission to exist and you start commanding the space you occupy. You feel me? So, how are you feeling?

She Designed Herself on Purpose

There is a massive difference between surviving a life and designing one. Survival is reactionary. It's what happens when you spend your days managing everyone else's comfort, rounding off your edges so no one gets nicked, and turning your own brightness down so no one has to look away. It's exhausting. But design? Design is an intentional act of authority.

I've lived in the gap between who I am and who people decided I was. I've sat in rooms where my truth took up more space than they were willing to make for it. There was a time I thought I had to humble myself just to be accepted. But I realized that humbling yourself for the sake of others is actually a form of self-sabotage. True humility is being your authentic self and loving yourself for what you are about to become, regardless of who stays for the transition. The woman she was becoming didn't happen because everything went right; she happened because I decided to take the raw materials of my failures, my heartbreaks, and my silences and turn them into a standard.

Desirability was never about winning someone else's vote. It's about deciding your own attention is the only currency you're interested in spending. Stop auditing your worth through other people's eyes and start auditing it through your own results. You start investing your time, your energy, and your focus the way you'd invest money—carefully, intentionally, and never in something with no return.

This isn't about becoming someone new. It's about finally collecting on who you already were. You stop showing up hoping to be considered and start showing up already holding the deed.

And once you own something outright, you stop asking permission to use it. You stop seeking outside approval for decisions that were always yours to make. People can admire the property all they want—they can stand outside the gate and comment on the landscaping—but ownership means you're the only one with a key. You decide who gets let in, what gets built next, and what gets torn down because it no longer serves the life you're protecting. That's not arrogance. That's just what it looks like when a woman finally reads her own paperwork.

The Aesthetic Is the Argument

Your life is a visual and energetic testament to what you believe about yourself. People think "aesthetic" is just about clothes or home decor, but I'm telling you, it's deeper than that. Your aesthetic is your boundary. It's the vibe you put out that tells the world exactly how you expect to be treated without you ever having to open your mouth.

Throughout this journey, I've learned that the most

dangerous woman in the room is the one who finally knows her worth. She doesn't have to prove it. When you transition into the woman you were becoming, your aesthetic changes. It becomes more edited. You stop carrying excess baggage—spiritually, emotionally, and physically.

If you find yourself still trying to convince people that you're valuable, you haven't fully stepped into your new build yet. You're still living in the construction zone. The finished product doesn't argue. A diamond doesn't argue its hardness; it just cuts glass. A crown doesn't explain why it's on a head; it just sits there. When you decide to be the standard, your very existence becomes the argument. People will either rise to meet you or they will fall away, and you have to be okay with the falling. The right people, the right opportunities, and the right rooms will never require you to be less. They will recognize the glitz of the diamonds on your crown and know exactly why they are there. Stop apologizing for the high-end frequency you're broadcasting. If they can't hear you, it's because their receiver is broken, not because your signal is weak.

She Became the Reference Point

For a long time, you probably looked to other women to understand how to be. You looked at the magazines, the influencers, or the "successful" women in your family and tried to piece together a version of yourself that fit. But when you arrive at the stage of the woman you were becoming, you stop looking for a reference point and you become one.

You realize that there is someone just like you who is looking up. Someone who needs to see a woman who didn't just survive rock bottom but used it to build a palace. You become the shoulder for others because you've had to be your own. This isn't about being perfect; it's about being certain.

Being the reference point means you define the terms. You don't ask what the market rate for your time is; you set the standard. You don't ask how much space you're allowed to take up; you occupy it. This is the unapologetic self. This is the woman who knows that her value is non-negotiable and her energy is a privilege. You aren't the same woman who started this book. You shouldn't be. You've been sharper, more intentional, and more edited with every chapter. You didn't just find your way; you paved it.

So, as you step out of these pages and into the world, remember that the standard isn't something you reach for—it's something you are. You are the banquet. You are the frequency. You are the architect of the woman you see in the mirror. Don't you ever dim yourself down to make someone else feel comfortable. If they can't handle your volume, let them buy earplugs. You didn't come back. You arrived.

Takeaway

Your identity is a deliberate creation, not a discovery. Stop seeking permission to be yourself and start setting the standard for how the world must meet you. You are the architect, the builder, and the resident of your own worth. Now go out there and live like you mean it.

CHAPTER 9

Money Moves Like She Does

A woman's relationship with money is inseparable from her relationship with herself. Undercharging, over-giving, and scarcity thinking are rooted in beliefs about worth, not financial literacy. When she does the internal work, her financial life shifts.

Money Moves Like She Does

If you want to see how a woman feels about herself, don't look at her jewelry—look at her invoices. Look at how she handles a bill, how she asks for a raise, and how quickly she discounts her magic because she's afraid of being 'too expensive' for people with cheap mindsets. We've been told that money is just math, a cold transaction of numbers and decimals. But I'm telling you, money is a mirror. It is a reflection of the Standard you have set for your own life. You feel me? For most women over forty, thinking about money brings up a specific kind of tightness in the chest. It's not because you aren't capable; it's because you've been trained to view money as a measure of your worthiness rather than a tool for your vision.

I've been the woman who over-delivered and under-charged. I've been the one who felt guilty for wanting more, as if my ambition was a betrayal of my character. But the most dangerous woman in the room is the one who finally knows her worth and realizes that her financial state is the direct result of her internal state. Money doesn't just show up because you work hard; it shows up because you believe you are a destination for it. It moves like you do—with authority, with intention, and with a complete lack of apology. If you are still shrinking yourself to be 'affordable,' you aren't just losing dollars; you are losing the very essence of your power.

Her Relationship with Money Was Always Personal

We have to stop pretending that our financial struggles are just about a lack of information. We live in the information age. You can find a million videos on how to save, invest, and budget. But if information were the only thing we needed, we'd all be millionaires with six-pack abs. The reason the math doesn't add up is that the spirit is out of alignment. Your relationship with money is inseparable from your relationship with yourself. Every time you hesitate to charge what you're worth, every time you let a client slide on a payment, every time you spend money you don't have to impress people you don't even like—that is your trauma talking, not your bank.

I had to learn that scarcity isn't a lack of resources; it's a mindset of lack. If you grew up like I did, seeing women who were always 'just getting by' or who had to ask permission for every penny they spent, that script is etched into your subconscious. You start to believe that being a 'good' woman means being a struggling woman. You think that humility and poverty are siblings. Let me tell you: they aren't even related. Real humility is knowing who you are and what you bring to the table. Real humility is being able to command a high price because you know the high value of your impact.

When I was building my own path, I had to learn that my ambition wasn't up for a vote. I stopped waiting for someone to tell me it was acceptable to want more. It wasn't about being greedy; it was about being free. Wealth is the ability to say 'no' without worrying about how you'll eat. Wealth is the ability to walk away from a toxic room because your rent isn't tied to their respect. If you are constantly operating from a place of 'enough,' you will never reach the level of 'excess' where you can actually change the world. You've been trying to solve a spiritual problem with a spreadsheet. You have to start desiring your future more than you fear the judgment of people who are comfortable with your struggle.

She Built Something That Was Hers

There is a specific kind of dignity that comes from building something that nobody can take away from you. For too many years, women have been told to invest in everyone else's dreams. You've invested in your husband's career, your children's education, your boss's company, and your friends' drama. You've been the ultimate support system, the invisible scaffolding that keeps everyone else standing. But what have you built that belongs exclusively to you? What is the asset that carries your signature?

The woman who is the Standard knows that her energy is her greatest currency. When I started building my brand, it wasn't just about a logo or a catchy tagline; it was about constructing something solid enough to hold my future. I decided I wasn't waiting for a seat anywhere—I was building the whole table myself. I didn't want a seat at a table where I'd have to beg for a crumb; I wanted to own the room where the table sits. This requires shift from being an employee of your life to being the CEO of your soul.

You have to be the architect of your own security. This means you stop asking 'What can I get?' and start asking 'What can I build?' Whether it's a business, a brand, an investment portfolio, or a legacy of knowledge, it has to be yours. I've seen so many women hit forty or fifty and realize they've spent their best years building someone else's empire, only to be left with nothing when the empire decides they are no longer 'useful.' That will not be your story. When you build something that is yours, you aren't just making money; you are making a statement. You are saying that your ideas have weight and your vision has value. You aren't just surviving; you are arriving. And when you arrive as the owner, you don't have to explain your presence. The deed is the only argument you need.

She Priced Herself Correctly

If I could give every woman one gift, it would be the courage to stop discounting her soul. We have been socialized to be 'reasonable.' We want to be accessible. We want people to like us, so we 'meet them where they are' by lowering our rates, our standards, and our expectations. Let me tell you why that's a trap: when you lower your price to fit someone's budget, you also lower the level of respect they have for your work. People don't value what doesn't cost them anything.

I've lived that life where I was speaking truth and felt I had to be quiet about my worth. I thought I had to humble myself so people wouldn't think I was 'all about the money.' But here is the contrarian truth: The right people—the ones who are supposed to be in your world—will never ask you for a discount. They will see the Standard you set and they will meet it, because they understand that they aren't just paying for your time; they are paying for the years of pain, transition, and evolution it took for you to become the woman who can solve their problem in five minutes.

Pricing yourself correctly is a form of discernment. It's the ultimate filter. When you set a high price, you aren't being 'difficult'—you're being clear. You are telling the world that your time is a luxury good. I remember the first time I raised my rates. My hands were shaking. I was terrified everyone would leave. And you know what? Some people did leave. But the people who stayed? They were the ones who truly valued my energy. They were the ones who didn't drain me. By pricing myself correctly, I actually created more peace in my life.

You have to realize that you are a high-value asset. You aren't a commodity; you are a category of one. When you treat yourself like a discount brand, you attract discount problems. When you treat yourself like a premium experience, you attract premium opportunities. Stop looking at what everyone else is charging and start looking at what your peace is worth. If taking a client means you lose your sleep, they can't afford you. If taking a job means you have to dim your light, the salary isn't high enough. The Standard doesn't negotiate with scarcity. You set the price, you hold the line, and you let the world adjust to your frequency.

Takeaway

Your net worth will never outgrow your self-worth. If you want more in your bank, you have to start by wanting more for yourself. Money is just energy, and energy follows the Standard. Stop asking for permission to be prosperous and start commanding the value you know you provide. Once you've mastered the flow of your resources, you're ready for the ultimate test: ensuring that the trail you leave behind is one that others can actually follow.

CHAPTER 10

The Other Women Watching.

The most dangerous woman in the room is the one who understands her presence is a curriculum for the next generation. Your legacy isn't your logo or your bank account—it's the permission you give every woman watching to finally stop shrinking and start standing.

You think you're just living your life, but you're actually writing a manual. Every time you set a boundary without stuttering, every time you walk away from a table where respect isn't being served, and every time you choose your peace over a performance, someone is watching. Maybe it's your daughter, observing the way you handle a man who doesn't value you. Maybe it's the woman in the cubicle next to yours, wondering how you got the nerve to say no to that extra work. Or maybe it's the woman you used to be, peering through the glass of your progress. The Standard was never meant to be a private club of one. It is a lighthouse. And the thing about a lighthouse is that it doesn't have to shout to be seen; it just has to keep its light steady so others don't crash against the rocks. You feel me? So, how are you feeling? Because once you realize that your healing is a catalyst for someone else's freedom, you stop playing small for the sake of their comfort.

how some become jealous- when they don't have to, it's plenty out here for us all

We have to talk about the 'green-eyed monster' in the room. When a woman starts to live by the Standard, she often expects the world to applaud. But sometimes, the loudest sound she hears is the sharpening of knives from the people she thought would be her biggest fans. I've seen it happen more times than I can count: a woman levels up, she starts owning her worth, she stops explaining herself, and suddenly, the whispers start. "She thinks she's better than us." "Who does she think she is?" "She's changed."

Let's be clear: jealousy is just a confession of perceived lack. When someone is jealous of you, they aren't actually mad at your success; they are mad at the mirror you're holding up to their own unfulfilled potential. Your light is bothering their eyes because they've become comfortable living in the dark. I learned early on that I had to humble myself—not by shrinking, but by realizing that their reaction to my growth was none of my business. I had to be quiet and let them sit with their own discomfort.

There is this toxic myth in our culture that there is only one seat at the table for a 'powerful woman.' It's the Highlander mentality—there can only be one. But that is a lie designed to keep us competing instead of collaborating. There is plenty out here for us all. The universe isn't a pie with a finite number of slices. It's an ocean. Me catching a big fish doesn't mean your net is going to come up empty. My desirability, my success, and my peace do not come at the expense of yours. When you see a woman winning, that's not a sign that you're losing; it's a sign that it's possible. If she can do it, the Standard is already in the atmosphere. Reach up and grab your piece. Stop looking at her plate and start seasoning your own.

how we can be so powerful if we just work together

Imagine the frequency of a room where no one is trying to

prove they belong because everyone already knows they do. Imagine a sisterhood where we stop auditing each other's choices and start protecting each other's peace. That is where real power lives. We are formidable individually, but we are a force of nature when we align. I've spent years realizing that I don't need a seat at every table, but I definitely need to know who is sitting at the tables next to mine.

We've been conditioned to be suspicious of one another. We've been taught that every other woman is a threat to our territory, our man, or our career. But the Standard woman knows that her territory is her soul, and no one can take that. When you are secure in your own skin, you don't have to look at another woman as a rival. You look at her as a teammate. I don't mind being someone's shoulder, because the truth is, we all need that support sometimes. But there's a difference between being a shoulder and being a crutch. We work together when we hold each other to the Standard.

Working together means I don't let you settle. It means if I see you shrinking, I call you back into your greatness. It means we share the blueprints. If I found a way to the other side of heartbreak or a way to build a brand that sustains my spirit, I'm not going to gatekeep that information. I'm going to pass the baton. There is a specific kind of magic that happens when women stop competing and start co-creating. We can change the entire temperature of a community, a business, or a family when we decide that my win is our win. The most dangerous woman in the room is the one who brings other dangerous women with her.

you don't need a man to abuse you to feel, validated.

This is a hard truth, and I'm going to say it plainly: many of us have been taught to equate intensity with intimacy. We've been conditioned to think that if he isn't checking our phones, getting jealous, or causing 'good' trouble, then he doesn't really want us. We've mistaken control for care and chaos for passion. We've lived in cycles of 'make-up to break up' because the adrenaline of the fight made us feel seen. But let me tell you something from the bottom of my heart: you do not need to be mistreated to be significant.

I've been the woman who thought being 'chosen' by a difficult man was a prize. I thought if I could be the one to change him, the one to survive his moods, or the one to endure his disrespect, it proved that I was special. It didn't. It just proved I didn't know my own value yet. Validation that comes from a place of struggle is just a performance of pain. Real desirability—the kind we've been talking about since chapter one—is silent. It doesn't need a man to abuse you or 'test' you to know that you are the prize.

If you find yourself staying in a situation where your spirit is being chipped away, ask yourself: *What part of me believes this is what I deserve?* You do not need his drama to feel alive. You do not need his approval to feel beautiful. And you certainly do not need his permission to be the Standard. When you realize that your worth is non-negotiable, you stop being an option for someone who treats you like an accessory. You are the banquet. If he can't appreciate the spread, let him go find a snack somewhere else. You aren't leaving because you're angry—though you might be—you're leaving because you've finally realized that your presence is too expensive for a discount heart.

Takeaway

Your life is the script that the women around you are reading to learn how to treat themselves. By holding the Standard, you aren't just saving your own life; you're providing the navigation for everyone else coming behind you. You are the ancestor they've been waiting for. Now that you know you aren't the problem, it's time to realize you've always been the solution. In the final chapter, we'll see that the woman you've been searching for has been there the whole time.

EPILOGUE

She Already Was

She Already Was

You've been running toward a woman you thought was miles ahead of you, only to realize she was the one holding your hand the entire time. You feel me? We spend decades thinking that the "Standard" is a peak we have to climb, a status we have to earn, or a version of ourselves that only exists once we've fixed every perceived flaw. We treat our evolution like a construction site—all dust, noise, and blueprints for a future that hasn't arrived yet. But here is the truth that will quiet the room: You didn't become a queen. You just stopped pretending you weren't one.

The most dangerous woman in the room is the one who finally knows her worth, but the most powerful woman is the one who realizes she never actually lost it. You haven't been building a new woman from scratch; you've been excavating her. You've been peeling back the layers of "should" and "musts" that the world piled onto you until you were buried under everyone else's expectations. Every chapter we've walked through, every boundary you've set, and every silence you've honored wasn't adding something new to your soul—it was removing the clutter that prevented you from seeing what was already there. You were never broken, baby. You were just covered up. So, how are you feeling? Because from where I'm standing, you look like a woman who just remembered who she is.

The Remembering: It Was Never About Becoming

We love a good transformation story. We've been sold the "before and after" photos, the radical life-overhaul, and the idea that we have to be "reborn" to be valuable. But a comeback is just a return to a state that was already yours. When I look back at the moments, I felt most lost—when I was quiet because I was afraid my truth would ruffle feathers, or when I was striving for validation from people who didn't even know themselves—I wasn't a different person. I was just a woman who had forgotten her own name. I was a woman who had misplaced her crown and was looking for it in everyone else's pockets.

The work we've done together in this book isn't about "becoming" something you aren't. It's about the Great Remembering. It's that moment of clarity when the fog of forty years lifts and you realize that the fire, the grit, the discernment, and the high standards were in your DNA from day one. Think back to that little girl you used to be—the one before she was told her laugh was too loud, her questions were too much, or her dreams were too big. She knew she was the standard. She didn't ask if she could sit at the table; she just sat down. She didn't wait for a seat to be offered; she assumed the room was hers because she was in it.

Real self-worth is silent because it's ancient. It's not a new trend you picked up in a seminar. It's the original factory setting of your spirit. When you stop trying to "become" and start simply "being," the exhaustion vanishes. You realize that you don't need to perform for an audience that isn't qualified to judge the show. You don't have to prove your value to a world that profits from you feeling worthless. When I finally humbled myself and decided to just be my authentic self, I didn't find a new Shareta. I found the one I had been hiding from the world out of some misplaced sense of politeness. I realized I didn't need to be "more"; I just needed to be "me" without the apologies. The standard isn't a goal. It's an origins story.

The Unapologetic Mirror: Seeing Your Own Reflection for the First Time

Most women look in the mirror and see a list of things to fix. They see the evidence of the years, the marks of the battles they've fought, and the features that don't fit the current aesthetic of a society obsessed with youth. But when you are the Standard, your mirror changes. You stop looking for what's missing and you start seeing what's present. You start seeing a woman who has survived every 100% of her worst days. You see a woman whose body has been a vessel for miracles, heartbreaks, and resurrections. You see a woman who no longer needs a second opinion on her own existence.

I've spent a lot of time in front of that mirror, peeling back the lies. I learned that knowing exactly what you will and will not accept; it's the way you honor the reflection looking back at you. If you do not love the woman in the mirror, you will spend your whole life auditioning for people who cannot save you. And no amount of praise will fix it. No follower counts. No relationship. No validation from someone who has not even decided who they are yet. You cannot outsource the work of becoming — and you cannot borrow someone else's eyes to see yourself clearly.

Desirability is not assigned. It is not given to you by the way someone looks at you across a room. It is built — quietly, deliberately — in the moments you choose yourself when no one is watching. In the morning you wake up and decide today looks different. In the boundary you hold even when your hands are shaking. In the life you start craving so deeply that you finally stop waiting for someone else to hand it to you.

The mirror is not the enemy. She never was. The woman looking back at you has been waiting — patient, steady, certain — for you to finally see what she already knows.

When you can look at her and feel pulled toward her — her stillness, her power, the life she is walking into — you have not almost arrived.

You are already there.

This is the point where you stop negotiating with your reflection. You stop asking, "Is this enough?" and you start asserting, "This is it." All those years you made yourself smaller so the room could breathe easier — you understand now what those moments actually were. Not failures. Not evidence that you were too much. They were rehearsals. Every time you dimmed yourself to keep the peace, you were learning exactly what peace was costing you. Every time you were misunderstood for being exactly who you were, you were being refined — not rejected.

Being palatable was never the goal. It was the prison.

The purple. The gold. The crown. The diamonds. None of it was ever about impressing anyone. Those are not decorations. They are declarations. They are the external language of something she decided internally — that she was done denying what she already was. Royalty is not a title someone grants you. It is a truth you either live by or spend your whole life running from.

Your reflection was never a project waiting to be completed.

She has been finished for a long time — layered, intentional, undeniable. You were not building her. You were just finally letting yourself see her. You turned the lights on. And what was already there — what was always there — took your breath away.

That is not a beginning.

That is a recognition.

Living the Standard: No More Auditions, Just Final Acts

We are done auditioning. You feel me? The season of trying out for roles in other people's lives is officially closed. You are no longer the understudy in your own story. When you live as the standard, you realize that your life isn't a series of tests to see if you're worthy; it's a series of experiences where you decide who is worthy of *you*. This shift in perspective is the ultimate power move. It's the difference between being a guest and being the host. Between being the banquet and being the person begging for a crumb.

Living the standard means your energy is curated. Your inner circle is edited. Your "No" is heavy and your "Yes" is rare. You don't have to shout about your boundaries because they are built into the way you move. People feel the velvet rope before they even get close enough to touch it. This isn't about being cold; it's about being clear. The right rooms do not require an audition.

The right people will not make you justify your presence or shrink your energy to make the introduction easier. The right opportunities will not arrive with conditions attached to your worthiness. When alignment is real — when the room, the person, the moment is actually meant for you — there is no proving. There is only arriving. And the difference between the two will become one of the clearest things you have ever felt.

But some rooms will not rise to meet you. Some people will stay exactly where you left them — standing at the bottom, still referencing a version of you that no longer exists. Still telling the story of who you were as though it is evidence of who you are. Let them. The woman still climbing does not stop to correct the narrative of everyone watching from below. She does not owe anyone a defense. She does not owe anyone an explanation.

And she does not owe anyone a hand back down.

Some people were never meant to come with you. They were meant to watch. To witness. To one day point at the distance between where you are and where you started — and understand, finally, what the standard always was.

You keep climbing.

Not to prove anything.

Because the view from where you are going is nothing like anything they can see from where they are standing.

The woman on the other side of this book is not the same woman who opened the first page. She is sharper. She is more intentional. She is unbothered. She knows that going back is the wrong goal entirely. You didn't survive everything you went through just to return to who you were. You survived it so you could arrive at who you are. The standard is now your baseline, not your ceiling. You don't have to work to maintain it; you just have to refuse to drop below it.

You were always her. Through the tears, through the rock bottoms, through the periods of being quiet and the periods of being too loud for the small-minded—you were always the standard. You just had to decide to agree with God about who He made you to be. You had to decide that you were worth the investment of your own attention. As you close this book and walk out into a world that will try to remind you of your old labels, I want you to remember one thing: You didn't change. You just stopped hiding.

Takeaway

The Standard was never a destination you had to reach—it was the truth you had to stop denying. You didn't become the woman of your dreams; you just woke up and realized you were already her. Now, go into every room and every relationship with the quiet authority of someone who has nothing left to prove and everything to enjoy. The banquet is set, and it's all for you. You feel me? So, how are you feeling now?

About the Author

Shareta Cunningham — creator of Desirable LaRue — built her world without a blueprint, without a mentor, and without waiting for permission. As a creator, author, and brand architect, she has spent years building at the intersection of luxury aesthetics, AI-powered storytelling, and unapologetic self-expression. She is the founder and sole architect of Desirable LaRue — a women's empowerment brand where faith, femininity, and unbothered authority live in the same breath.

Everything she has built, she built herself. Not because she had to — but because she understood that the most powerful thing a woman can own is something that is entirely hers.

The Standard is her most direct work yet — and she lived every word of it. The unraveling. The deciding. The rebuilding. The arriving. She wrote it for the woman who can feel the standard inside of her but has not yet given herself permission to live by it. Because someone needed to say it plainly — desirability was never something to earn. It was always something to decide.

The most dangerous woman in the room is the one who finally knows her worth. You feel me? So, how are you feeling? desirablelarue.com

www.ingramcontent.com/pod-product-compliance
Lightning Source LLC
LaVergne TN
LVHW010738061126
851857LV00014B/1537
* 9 7 9 8 2 3 4 1 5 7 0 9 6 *